Cummins and Scoullar's

The Little Prince
the play
~large-cast version~

by
Rick Cummins and John Scoullar

Adapted from the book
by
Antoine de Saint-Exupéry

Dramatic Publishing
Woodstock, Illinois • England • Australia • New Zealand

*** NOTICE ***

The amateur and stock acting rights to this work are controlled exclusively by THE DRAMATIC PUBLISHING COMPANY without whose permission in writing no performance of it may be given. Royalty fees are given in our current catalog and are subject to change without notice. Royalty must be paid every time a play is performed whether or not it is presented for profit and whether or not admission is charged. A play is performed any time it is acted before an audience. All inquiries concerning amateur and stock rights should be addressed to:

DRAMATIC PUBLISHING
P. O. Box 129, Woodstock, Illinois 60098

COPYRIGHT LAW GIVES THE AUTHOR OR THE AUTHOR'S AGENT *THE EXCLUSIVE RIGHT TO MAKE COPIES.* This law provides authors with a fair return for their creative efforts. Authors earn their living from the royalties they receive from book sales and from the performance of their work. Conscientious observance of copyright law is not only ethical, it encourages authors to continue their creative work. This work is fully protected by copyright. No alterations, deletions or substitutions may be made in the work without the prior written consent of the publisher. No part of this work may be reproduced or transmitted in any form or by any means, electronic or mechanical, including photocopy, recording, videotape, film, or any information storage and retrieval system, without permission in writing from the publisher. It may not be performed either by professionals or amateurs without payment of royalty. All rights, including but not limited to the professional, motion picture, radio, television, videotape, foreign language, tabloid, recitation, lecturing, publication and reading, are reserved.

©MM by
RICK CUMMINS and JOHN SCOULLAR

Adapted from the book by
ANTOINE DE SAINT-EXUPÉRY

Printed in the United States of America
All Rights Reserved
(THE LITTLE PRINCE, the play, large-cast version)

ISBN 1-58342-005-3

IMPORTANT BILLING AND CREDIT REQUIREMENTS

All producers of the Play *must* give credit to the Author(s) of the Play in all programs distributed in connection with performances of the Play and in all instances in which the title of the Play appears for purposes of advertising, publicizing or otherwise exploiting the Play and/or a production. The name of the Author(s) *must* also appear on a separate line, on which no other name appears, immediately following the title, and *must* appear in size of type not less than fifty percent the size of the title type. Specific credit must be given as follows:

(50%)   Cummins and Scoullar's
(100%)   THE LITTLE PRINCE
                      by
(50%)   Rick Cummins and John Scoullar

(25%) Based on the book by Antoine de Saint-Exupéry
(10%)   Copyright © 1943 and renewed 1971 by
              Harcourt Brace & Co.

Originally produced off-Broadway by Chrysalis Productions at the John Houseman Theatre Complex. Earlier version produced and directed by Michael Harron at Playhouse by the River, Mt. Bethel, Pa.

On all programs this notice should appear:

"Produced by special arrangement with
THE DRAMATIC PUBLISHING COMPANY of Woodstock, Illinois"
* * * *

Note: Printed material, including playbooks and music, whether used for perusal or for the production of the play or musical version of THE LITTLE PRINCE, is provided strictly on a rental basis. All material must be returned to Dramatic Publishing upon completion of its use.

AUTHORS' NOTE

This large-cast version of *The Little Prince* utilizes a special stage ensemble of 6-8 actors. We envision these actors dressed inconspicuously (e.g., in black unitards and head coverings), moving in subtle stylized fashion, and using various simple props. The ensemble should become "human scenery," inspiring the audience to see the illusions they create without drawing attention to themselves as individuals. As indicated in the script, they can help create the illusion of flight, glorious sunsets, starry skies, and windswept sand dunes. They can facilitate the appearance of volcanoes, baobabs, trees, and wheat fields. The script indications are our staging suggestions. Use them as they are or elaborate on them if you wish. When used tastefully and sparingly, they can be effective and fun. Remember, less is more. Have fun and "break a leg!"

THE LITTLE PRINCE

A Full-length Play With Optional Intermission
For up to 32 actors

CHARACTERS

Aviator
Little Prince
Rose
King
Conceited Man
Businessman
Lamplighter
Geographer
Snake
Desert Flower
Fox
Sketch Artist
Special Stage Ensemble (6-8)
Optional extra roses for the Wall of Roses (12)

THE LITTLE PRINCE

AT RISE: *The ENSEMBLE is in place, holding multi-branched sticks dotted with small lights and/or "stars" of different sizes, creating a starry frame around the projection screen.*

(Projection screen fades up. [Tape Cue #1] An ethereal solo voice sings as a hand is seen making a simple drawing. See Illustration B.)

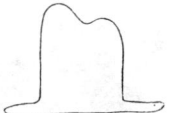

When it is completed, lights come up on AVIATOR, pencil in hand, admiring the drawing on his pad, which we are to assume is the same as the one on the screen. AVIATOR addresses the audience as though imparting a great confidence.

AVIATOR. When I was six years old, once upon a very long time ago, I made this drawing. I showed my masterpiece to the grown-ups and asked, "Does it frighten you?" But they said, "Why should anyone be frightened by a hat?" It was not a hat. So I drew it for them more clearly. Grown-ups always need to have things explained to them.

([Tape Cue #2] As he draws, the hand in the projection sketches again. See Illustration C.)

It was a boa constrictor having swallowed an elephant. But this time they said, "Put those crayons away and study arithmetic or geography or something *important.*" So I did... but I always kept my first drawing with me as a test of true understanding.

([Tape Cue #3] The first drawing reappears. See Illustration B.)

AVIATOR. But no matter who I showed it to, they would always say, "That is a hat." So I threw it away and I never again spoke to them about boa constrictors, or primeval forests, or stars. And I never again made another drawing. *(Crumples drawing in fist. Illustration B off.)* I learned to pilot airplanes.

([Tape Cue #4] Sound of plane is heard. If no set piece is used for plane, drawing of plane comes up. See Illustration D. During the next line, AVIATOR dons a scarf and aviator hat and sits either in the plane or on a stool in front of the projected drawing. As he sits, the ENSEMBLE's stars move and surround the plane.)

And I lived my life alone... until six years ago, when I had an accident with my plane in the Desert of Sahara.

(There is thunder and lightning. AVIATOR is in a storm. Coordinated movement of the stars may help demonstrate the turbulence of the storm.)

Whoa! Hold on there, my friend. Where are we? Somewhere over the Sahara, I imagine. *(More turbulence.)* Or some otherwhere. *(Engine sputters.)* What's the matter

THE LITTLE PRINCE – the play

with you? *(More sputtering.)* Looks like I'm going to have to take you down. *(Plane swoops. AVIATOR speaks into radio.)* Come in, Tangiers. Tangiers, come in. This is Solitaire. *(Storm escalates.)* Somebody! Anybody! Come in! Isn't anybody there? Solitaire going down for emergency landing. Making emergency landing approximately— *(Engine stops. Plane begins to descend.)* Woooo— *(He force lands in a confusion of lights as the ENSEMBLE exits by scattering off the stage and Illustration D (if used) fades out. Music continues.)*

BLACKOUT

(Lights up slowly on AVIATOR asleep on the sand and then revealing the LITTLE PRINCE behind a scrim.)

LITTLE PRINCE. Please, sir, draw me a sheep. *(Music ends.)*

AVIATOR *(sits up suddenly as if from a nightmare)*. What! *(He sees nothing. AVIATOR gets up slowly, walks around getting his bearings. He is confused. The LITTLE PRINCE appears again elsewhere behind scrim.)*

LITTLE PRINCE. Draw me a sheep.

AVIATOR *(turns, spots him, and heads toward him)*. Hello! Hello— Who are you?— Where— *(LITTLE PRINCE has vanished. AVIATOR is at a loss. He looks fearfully around him.)* Where are we? *(Standing in place, he winces as he feels sand in his boot. Removing it, he pours sand out. With understanding, and relieved, if cynical, resignation:)* Something tells me this isn't the Riviera. *(AVIATOR goes to plane, remembering.)* Ah yes, the storm...the engine trouble...the radio...*the radio! (He goes to the radio.)* Come in, Tangiers! Do you read me? Cairo, come in! Somebody! (He discovers radio cord is severed and slams down headset.) Damn!

(LITTLE PRINCE has now entered, pad and pencil in hand, standing atop a dune.)

LITTLE PRINCE. If you please, draw me a sheep.
AVIATOR *(taken back and totally confused).* You—there—here—in the desert— But who— *(LITTLE PRINCE approaches. AVIATOR sits in weakness.)*
LITTLE PRINCE. Draw me a sheep.
AVIATOR *(after a beat, blankly).* I don't draw!
LITTLE PRINCE. You used to.
AVIATOR. How would you know—
LITTLE PRINCE *(firmly).* Draw me a sheep.
AVIATOR *(to audience).* When a mystery is too overpowering, one dares not disobey.

(Taking pad and pencil, the AVIATOR complies reluctantly. As he draws, the hand in the projection sketches AVIATOR's first drawing. See Illustration B. **[Tape Cue #5]** *AVIATOR hands his drawing to the LITTLE PRINCE.)*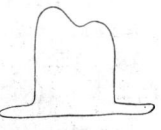

LITTLE PRINCE. No no no! I don't want an elephant inside a boa constrictor. A boa constrictor is very dangerous and an elephant is very large. I need a sheep. Draw me a sheep.

THE LITTLE PRINCE – the play

*(AVIATOR is shocked. As he flips page of pad up, artist removes Illustration B. AVIATOR reluctantly begins to draw again. See Illustration E. **[Tape Cue #6]** AVIATOR hands him the drawing.)*

LITTLE PRINCE. You can see for yourself that's not a sheep. It's a ram, see? It has horns.

*(AVIATOR, annoyed, flips page same as before. Artist removes Illustration E. AVIATOR tries again. See Illustration F. **[Tape Cue #7]** AVIATOR hands him another.)*

This one is too old. I want a sheep that will live a long time.

(Frustrated, AVIATOR grabs pad out of LITTLE PRINCE's hand. He takes a deep breath, flips the page as before. Artist removes Illustration F. AVIATOR draws with finality. See Illustration G.)

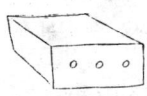

AVIATOR. This is a box. *(Handing drawing to LITTLE PRINCE.)* The sheep that you want is inside.
LITTLE PRINCE. That is exactly the way I wanted it! *(LITTLE PRINCE exits. Illustration G fades out.)*
AVIATOR *(to audience)*. And that was how I made the acquaintance of this strange little man.

*(**[Tape Cue #8]** AVIATOR goes to his plane. Music ends.)*

The next day, just before sunset, as I worked on my plane a thousand miles from any human habitation...

(LITTLE PRINCE enters.)

...he appeared again. It took me a long time to learn where he came from. This little person, who asked so many questions, never seemed to hear the ones I asked.

LITTLE PRINCE. It is true, isn't it? Sheep eat little bushes?
AVIATOR *(turns, startled)*. Where did you go yesterday?
LITTLE PRINCE. It is true, isn't it?
AVIATOR *(exasperated)*. Yes.
LITTLE PRINCE. Then it follows that they also eat baobabs, correct?
AVIATOR. Baobabs are not little bushes. They're trees as big as castles, and—
LITTLE PRINCE. But before they grow so big, the baobabs, they start out by being little?
AVIATOR. Strictly speaking, yes. Where is your family? Where do you come from? Why do you want the sheep to eat the little baobabs, anyway? *(LITTLE PRINCE doesn't answer, he has wandered over to plane.)* Don't you ever answer a question?
LITTLE PRINCE. What is this object?
AVIATOR *(turns, startled)*. That is not an object. That is my airplane...my—friend. *(With irony.)*
LITTLE PRINCE *(investigates the plane)*. Hello.
AVIATOR. It doesn't talk. It's true, I talk to it occasionally—but it doesn't answer back.

THE LITTLE PRINCE – the play

LITTLE PRINCE. That doesn't seem very satisfactory. *(LITTLE PRINCE is puzzled.)*
AVIATOR. It's an airplane! It flies!
LITTLE PRINCE. You dropped down from the sky?
AVIATOR. Yes. *(LITTLE PRINCE laughs. AVIATOR is miffed. LITTLE PRINCE tries to suppress his laughter.)* What's so funny?! *(LITTLE PRINCE bursts into laughter again. AVIATOR speaks to audience.)* His laughter irritated me. I liked my misfortunes taken seriously. *(With a look from the AVIATOR, LITTLE PRINCE contains his laughter.)*
LITTLE PRINCE. You too come from the sky. Which is your planet?
AVIATOR. What?
LITTLE PRINCE. Though it *is* true that on that airplane you couldn't have come very far.
AVIATOR. You come from another planet?
LITTLE PRINCE. Listen to that sunset. Do you hear the music?
AVIATOR. What music?
LITTLE PRINCE. It's wonderful that the sunset lasts such a long time here. Where I come from, the sunsets are much shorter, but there are so many more of them.
AVIATOR. It's clear I'm not going to get a straight answer out of you. I have to get back to my pl— *(AVIATOR heads back to plane.)*
LITTLE PRINCE. One day I watched the sun set forty-four times.
AVIATOR. Forty-four times?
LITTLE PRINCE *(takes his hand)*. Come with me.
AVIATOR *(pulling his hand away)*. Enough of this. I have important things to—

([Tape Cue #9] The lights abruptly change as the ENSEMBLE enters at the wings and instantly creates a magnificent evolving sunset, stopping AVIATOR mid-sentence. LITTLE PRINCE offers his hand to stunned AVIATOR.)

LITTLE PRINCE. Come.

(AVIATOR takes his hand and follows in awe as they walk through the sunset. [NOTE: ENSEMBLE could create this sunset through the use of shards of red, yellow, orange, and purple lightweight translucent fabric, waved like shredded banners or ribbons from wings on each side of the stage, in a Japanese Noh Theatre-like fashion. This would embellish a central glow of stage lighting—on the backdrop—as it changes colors and slowly descends.])

You see, where I come from, it is so small that all you need to do is move your chair a few steps and you can see the day end and the twilight fall as many times as you like. But here on your planet you can walk and walk and still be in the same magnificent sunset. *(They continue to walk.)* One loves the sunset when one is so sad.

AVIATOR. Were you so sad, then?
LITTLE PRINCE. I kept wondering what it was that I was missing and wishing I had. *(The sun has set, the ENSEMBLE esits, and the starry night sky fades up.)* So far away from home it's good to have someone to watch the sunset with. *(Music ends. LITTLE PRINCE is looking at his drawing.)* The thing that is so good about the box you've given me is that at night my sheep can use it as his house.

THE LITTLE PRINCE – the play

AVIATOR. And if you're good, I'll draw you a string and a post so you can tie him during the day.
LITTLE PRINCE. Tie him? What a strange idea!
AVIATOR. Well, he might run off.
LITTLE PRINCE. Run off? Where do you think he would go?
AVIATOR. Anywhere. Straight ahead.
LITTLE PRINCE *(laughs, pause)*. Straight ahead, nobody can go very far. *(The AVIATOR is puzzled. LITTLE PRINCE is starting to leave.)* Look for me tomorrow—just at sunset.
AVIATOR. But—why do you come only at sunset? *(LITTLE PRINCE leaves.)* And where do you think you're going? *(LITTLE PRINCE is gone.)* Look, I really don't intend to be here all that long— *(Mumbling to himself.)* Straight ahead, nobody can go very far. *(Calling after LITTLE PRINCE.)* What's that supposed to mean? *(Going to plane, he frantically checks it all over for damage. To plane:)* Come on, we'll find out what the matter is right now and leave this bizarre little episode behind us. We can do it. You can do it. You've never let me down before. *(Frustrated, he kicks the plane. He sits, perturbed and alone. [Tape Cue #10] The sound of a rattle is heard and we see the shadow of a snake.)*

BLACKOUT

(The sound trails off through the blackout. Lights come up on AVIATOR reviewing the supplies he takes from his knapsack.)

AVIATOR. Let's see now— *(He takes out a pastry.)* One half-eaten croissant. *(He nibbles.)* Stale. *(He puts it down and takes out some cheese.)* Some lovely cheese— *(He sniffs it. It is powerful.)* Ripe. *(He retrieves an unidentifiable object and examines it from a number of angles.)* Some—other thing. I'm sure if I'm here long enough I'll find it delectable. But I'm equally as sure that it's not going to come to that. *(To plane.)* Today you are going to be more cooperative. Right, my friend?

(LITTLE PRINCE appears. [Tape Cue #11] The sun begins to set.)

LITTLE PRINCE. Talking again to your friend who doesn't answer back? *(AVIATOR turns to LITTLE PRINCE startled. Then turns away and feigns disinterest.)*
AVIATOR *(dryly)*. Sunset so soon?
LITTLE PRINCE *(picks up canteen)*. What is this? *(Examining canteen.)*
AVIATOR. It's water. It's my survival, thank you. *(AVIATOR snatches it back.*
LITTLE PRINCE. On my journey, I met a man who sold pills to quench thirst. If you took one a week, you'd never need water.
AVIATOR. They could come in handy—you don't happen to have any, do you?
LITTLE PRINCE. If I were thirsty—I think I'd rather take a stroll to a spring of fresh water.
AVIATOR. That would be nice. *(Drinking, he stops, realizing he must ration.)* But, since there's no spring of fresh water here in the desert, and you don't have any of those

THE LITTLE PRINCE – the play 17

pills with you, I'd— How long have you been on this journey?
LITTLE PRINCE *(turning to AVIATOR).* Have you always been alone?
AVIATOR *(reacts to the abrupt change of subject, then decides to answer).* No...but I prefer it that way. *(AVIATOR goes to work on plane.)*
LITTLE PRINCE. Do you?
AVIATOR. What about you—you live alone on your—planet, and—
LITTLE PRINCE. Do you hear the music?
AVIATOR *(notices LITTLE PRINCE watching the sunset).* Music? Oh, *(sarcastically)* do you mean am I "listening to the sunset"? No. I don't hear any music.
LITTLE PRINCE. I *did.*
AVIATOR. Yes, I know. *You* hear the music.
LITTLE PRINCE. No. I lived alone. Until the dawn— *(AVIATOR is puzzled.)* After the night of forty-four sunsets— you remember. I realize now that was the day my journey really began.
AVIATOR. What is this journey you keep talking about?
LITTLE PRINCE. Until then, I had led a very well-ordered life—

(LITTLE PRINCE moves to a platform which, as he speaks, is transformed into his planet through lighting and the use of the ENSEMBLE as indicated.)

I'd wake up every morning with such a lot to do. I'd clean out my two volcanoes.

(LITTLE PRINCE stops and watches as ENSEMBLE members, from beneath the platform, push two small papier-mâché volcanoes through slits in the fabric which is covering small holes in the platform. The volcanoes sputter eruptions. This can be done with delightful effect by using a straw with powder.)

I have three, actually. *(The third volcano pops up, this time without an eruption.)* The third one is extinct but I clean it anyway. One never knows. Then there are the baobabs.

(An ENSEMBLE member simulates the appearance and growth of a baobab weed by poking his green-gloved hand, wrist-high, from under the platform through another fabric-covered hole in front of LITTLE PRINCE.)

AVIATOR. Ah yes, the baobabs.
LITTLE PRINCE. They burrow down so deeply... *(Another "baobab" pokes through to his left.)* ...and they spread their roots so wide... *(Two more "baobabs" poke through behind him and to his right, thus surrounding him. LITTLE PRINCE picks up a hoe from behind the platform and begins to dig as he continues to speak.)* ...that if I don't dig them up as soon as they appear, they could break my planet into pieces. *(As each baobab shakes and withers, LITTLE PRINCE grabs the fingers of each glove and pulls it off until he is left only with a pile of empty green gloves.)* It's very hard work. One day, however, when I'd finished, I felt— *(LITTLE PRINCE has gathered all the gloves.)* —well, that was the day of the forty-four sunsets. *(He drops the gloves out of sight behind the platform.)* Something was missing.

THE LITTLE PRINCE – the play

AVIATOR. Did you find the answer then? In the sunset?
LITTLE PRINCE. No. Not in the sunset, *[Tape Cue #12]* but in the dawn the next day. That morning, from a seed blown from who knows where, a small sprout appeared —and it was not like any of the other small sprouts on my planet.

(At the back of the platform, from behind, two pale-green-gloved hands, in prayer position, begin to ascend.)

So I watched it carefully. You see it could have been some new kind of baobab. *(The hands continue to ascend, arms and elbows pressed together. They are covered with full-length evening gloves, dotted with four foam thorns at the wrists and elbows.)* But soon it became clear —it was something entirely new— *(The hands separate gracefully, arms still together.)* It stopped growing and began to get ready to produce a flower... *(The arms separate, gradually revealing the head and torso of the ROSE.)* A flower—like no flower I'd ever seen before. It chose its colors carefully and adjusted its petals one by one. A mysterious and glorious creature. *(The ROSE sways gracefully as music builds.)* And then finally...just as the dawn rose— *(Music stops.)*

ROSE *(seeing her surroundings for the first time)*. Oh. *(Seeing LITTLE PRINCE for the first time.)* Oh.
LITTLE PRINCE. You are so beautiful...
ROSE. I am?
LITTLE PRINCE. Yes.
ROSE. Oh. Hmm...What is that?
LITTLE PRINCE. Beautiful? It's something pleasing to see.

ROSE. Oh. *(She sounds out the word.)* Beau-ti-ful. Huh. What's that?

LITTLE PRINCE. That's a volcano.

ROSE. Oh, it's beautiful!

LITTLE PRINCE. No, it's just a— *(A baobab pokes through nearby.)*

ROSE. And that? That's beautiful, too.

LITTLE PRINCE. No, that's a baobab. *(He rushes to pull up the baobab and tosses the glove behind the platform.)*

ROSE *(pointing)*. And that? And that? And that? *(Notices the curl in his hair.)* Oh. That's beautiful, too. There's so much to see here—

LITTLE PRINCE. You are the most beautiful flower—

ROSE. What's a flower?

LITTLE PRINCE. Why, you— You are a flower.

ROSE *(pleased)*. Oh.

LITTLE PRINCE. And you are the most beautiful one on my planet.

ROSE. There are other flowers here?

LITTLE PRINCE. Not unique like you. Unique—like nothing else in all the world!

ROSE. Is unique as good as beautiful?

LITTLE PRINCE. Oh, yes.

ROSE. Oh, good. *(She spreads her arms grandly, pricking him.*

LITTLE PRINCE. Ow!

ROSE. What's that?

LITTLE PRINCE. That's a thorn.

ROSE. Oh! I have quite a few. I will try to be more careful.

LITTLE PRINCE. That's all right. It didn't hurt, really. Not much anyway. I'm just so happy you are here with me.

ROSE *(points to herself)*. You and *(Points to LITTLE PRINCE.)* me.

THE LITTLE PRINCE – the play

LITTLE PRINCE. No, no. I'm you and you're me.
ROSE. This is very confusing.
LITTLE PRINCE *(laughs)*. It doesn't matter, really. As long as we are here together. *(He indicates with his finger.)* What is it?
ROSE. What's we?
LITTLE PRINCE. Well, that's you and me together. We're we.

(Their fingers touch. [Tape Cue #13] They gaze lovingly at each other for a moment.)

AVIATOR. Sounds like a pretty jolly life you had there.
LITTLE PRINCE. It was. *(As LITTLE PRINCE talks to AVIATOR, we see ROSE fixing her petals.)* She was beautiful, she was exciting, and she was someone to talk to...who answered back.
AVIATOR. Yes...well.
LITTLE PRINCE. We spent so many lovely times together. But as time went by, things changed.

(Two or three of the ENSEMBLE's green-gloved baobabs slowly start to reappear.)

AVIATOR. Sounds familiar. *(LITTLE PRINCE looks quizzically.)* My experience has been much the same with flowers I have known.
LITTLE PRINCE. She seemed to resent every moment I spent away from her tending to my chores.

(LITTLE PRINCE eliminates the closest baobab with ease, then starts digging at the more distant baobabs.

ROSE watches with growing impatience. Finally she tries to tempt him away with musical refrains.)

ROSE *(a cappella)*. LA-LA-LA-LA— *(LITTLE PRINCE smiles but continues working. She looks around for distraction and suddenly spies a caterpillar on her leaf.)* Eek!
LITTLE PRINCE. What is it?
ROSE. It's a monster crawling on me. *(She holds out her leaf to show him.)*
LITTLE PRINCE. Oh. It's just a caterpillar. They're really very marvelous creatures. One day it will turn into a beautiful butterfly. But if it upsets you, I'll take it away...in just a moment.
ROSE *(waits impatiently trying to think of another way to get his attention. She clears her throat. He looks up)*. I seem to be very dry. Do you think I might have a drink?
LITTLE PRINCE. Certainly. As soon as I get this last little baobab. *(She is annoyed. LITTLE PRINCE is having a hard time with one particular baobab. ROSE begins to cough, lightly at first, then more vociferously. During this, LITTLE PRINCE has begun to have a tug of war with the baobab, who has now grabbed his hoe. He gets the hoe away from it and rushes to ROSE's side.)* What is it?
ROSE *(coughing dramatically. Hoarsely)*. Water...
LITTLE PRINCE *(rushes to water her)*. Are you all right?
ROSE. Much better now. Thank you. *(They smile. LITTLE PRINCE heads back to his work.)* But, I am feeling a bit of a chill.
LITTLE PRINCE *(gets her a screen)*. Better? *(She nods. He tries to leave again to tend to the ever-menacing baobabs.)*

THE LITTLE PRINCE – the play 23

ROSE. Oh, but now it seems I'm terribly warm again. *(He takes the screen away and waters her again.)*

LITTLE PRINCE. And so it went— *[Tape Cue #14]* day after day—until finally I had to tell her. *(To ROSE.)* Don't you see, if I don't return to my work, the baobabs could become dangerous to you.

ROSE. Well, go back to your baobabs then, if they're so very important. *(LITTLE PRINCE is hurt and does not move.)* Go on. Go back to your precious weeds! *(With this she has flailed dramatically and pricked him with her thorns. She is embarrassed and turns away.)*

LITTLE PRINCE *(to AVIATOR)*. I was confused. She was so beautiful but she made me so upset. I didn't understand her. I had so many questions, but no one to ask. I had to find some answers. I had to— I had to leave. I cleaned out my volcanoes for the last time—even the extinct one. And then—

(ROSE watches sadly as he does the above parting tasks. He approaches ROSE with wind screen.)

LITTLE PRINCE. Goodbye. *(She does not answer.)* Goodbye.

ROSE. Take the screen away...please.

LITTLE PRINCE. But the wind—

ROSE. I don't really need it. The night air will do me good. I am a flower, after all.

LITTLE PRINCE. Here then, let me take that caterpillar away. I know how it upsets...

ROSE. No, no. Leave it. I suppose I must endure the presence of two or three caterpillars if I wish to be acquainted with the butterflies. It seems that they are very beautiful. And if not the caterpillars and the butterflies, who will I talk to? You'll be far away. And as for any larger creatures, I'm not afraid. I have my thorns— *(She exhibits them, just missing LITTLE PRINCE. She is embarrassed.)* —to protect me. *(After a moment.)* Don't linger like this. You've decided to go now—so— *(She doesn't watch as he begins to leave. Suddenly she turns to him.)* Of course, I...lov— *(She cannot say "love." She can look at him no longer and turns away.)* Goodbye.

(He leaves dejected and confused. Lights cross back to the desert. AVIATOR is drawing absent-mindedly in the sand.)

LITTLE PRINCE. That was the last time I saw her. *(Music ends.)* Is that my flower?

AVIATOR *(caught unawares, trying to hide it)*. It's just a doodle—

LITTLE PRINCE. You should doodle more often. Of course, she has more petals than that—and her stem is really longer—and she has four thorns, you remember.

AVIATOR. Listen, I told you—I don't draw. I've only ever drawn boa constrictors from the outside and boa constrictors from the inside and—

LITTLE PRINCE. It's all right. Children will understand.

AVIATOR. Children were never the problem. It was the grown-ups who couldn't see—

LITTLE PRINCE. It's really quite good—not so good as my sheep, of course—but if you keep trying, who knows? You could maybe be an artist instead of—

AVIATOR. Instead of what? Listen, I have work to do— important things—

THE LITTLE PRINCE – the play

LITTLE PRINCE. Important things?
AVIATOR. Yes, important things. And besides, isn't it about time for you to take your leave? The sun has set, after all.
LITTLE PRINCE. Tomorrow— *(He leaves. [Tape Cue #15] AVIATOR angrily wipes out sand drawing.)*
AVIATOR. How am I supposed to know the details of your flower anyway? More petals, longer stem... For all I know the damn thing could look like... Who cares what it looks like?

(A change comes over him. He notices the sketch pad, takes it from the plane and sits in the sand. Beat. He begins to draw the ROSE again, making adjustments—which we see in projection. See Illustration H. As the AVIATOR continues to draw—lengthening the stem, adding more petals and thorns—the projection gradually fades and the ROSE appears as AVIATOR imagines what happened on LITTLE PRINCE's planet after he left his ROSE.)

ROSE. I did the right thing, didn't I? Letting him go, making him leave? Why did I do that? Why did he do that? Couldn't you see? Didn't you know? Of course I love you.

(Crossfade from ROSE to AVIATOR as he draws. Illustration I fades up. He adds a tear to the picture as music ends. Crossfade to next day. The AVIATOR is working on his plane, LITTLE PRINCE holds the drawing of the ROSE and is looking at it.)

LITTLE PRINCE. It's much better now. Much better than yesterday.

AVIATOR *(turns, sees that LITTLE PRINCE has drawing).* That's not for you. Give me that.
LITTLE PRINCE. I see you made the stem longer, and you added the thorns, and... *(He sees the tear.)* ...a tear.
AVIATOR *(looks at picture).* Well, I thought she probably felt—sad.
LITTLE PRINCE. Yes. You're right, of course. But all I knew then was how I felt. I was too young to know how to love her. The fact is, I didn't understand anything at all. So—I flew away.

([Tape Cue #16] ENSEMBLE enters as "stars." When LITTLE PRINCE says "So—I flew away," music begins and they lift him and carry him in such a way as to make him appear to be riding on or flying among the stars. AVIATOR follows behind, pad and pencil in hand.)

I wandered from star to star. I drifted around the cosmos until I came upon an entire group of planets, each inhabited by only one man. The first one I came to was inhabited by a king seated upon a throne.

(KING enters. ENSEMBLE puts LITTLE PRINCE down. With their backs to the audience, they then frame the scene with their stars.)

He was clad in a robe of royal purple and ermine that almost entirely covered his planet. Though he had never seen me before, he recognized me immediately.

(Music ends. LITTLE PRINCE approaches KING who is wearing a long robe. He is benign and eccentric—not

THE LITTLE PRINCE – the play

unlike Charlie Ruggles or Ed Wynn. [NOTE: Even though AVIATOR occasionally makes comments in the following planets sequence, the Character Man hears them as coming from LITTLE PRINCE.])

KING. Ah! A subject! Approach that I may see you better. *(LITTLE PRINCE yawns.)* Tsk. Tsk. It is not proper to yawn in the presence of a king. I order you not to yawn.

LITTLE PRINCE. I can't help it. I've traveled a long way and I haven't had any sleep.

KING. Ah...then I order you to yawn. It's been years since I've seen anyone yawn. Yes, yes, give us a good one now. It's an order.

LITTLE PRINCE *(tries to, but can't)*. I'm sorry, I guess I can't anymore.

KING. Hmm, hmm... Then I— I order you to sometimes yawn and sometimes—not to yawn. There. You see, my orders are very reasonable, don't you think?

LITTLE PRINCE. May I sit down?

KING. I order you to sit down.

LITTLE PRINCE. Sir?

KING. Sire.

LITTLE PRINCE. Sire.

KING. Sure.

LITTLE PRINCE. Sire, excuse me for asking a question—

KING. I order you to ask me a question.

LITTLE PRINCE. Over what do you rule?

KING. Over everything.

AVIATOR. Everything?

KING *(gesturing towards the universe)*. Everything.

LITTLE PRINCE. And the stars obey you?

KING. Certainly they do—and the moon and sun as well.

LITTLE PRINCE. Oh. *(Amazed, he asks timidly.)* Well, then, if you please, sire—could you possibly order a sunset? I should love to see a sunset.

KING. And so you shall!

LITTLE PRINCE *(settles in expectation but nothing happens)*. When?

KING. Oh, soon, soon. I shall command it. But I have to wait for conditions to be favorable.

LITTLE PRINCE. When do you think that will be?

KING. Oh, mm, *(Checks watch.)* I'd say—this evening about twenty to eight. You'll see how well I am obeyed.

LITTLE PRINCE. Excuse me, but I should be going—

KING. Oh, don't go, don't go. I'll make you a minister of justice.

LITTLE PRINCE. But there's no one here to judge.

KING. Then you shall judge yourself. That is the most difficult thing of all...

LITTLE PRINCE. Judge myself...?

KING. It is much more difficult to judge oneself than to judge others.

([Tape Cue #17] KING exits as ENSEMBLE lifts LITTLE PRINCE to have him "fly" with the stars. Illustration J fades up as AVIATOR draws final touches while following beside them.)

LITTLE PRINCE *(to AVIATOR)*. Then I knew it might be of some value to visit the other planets as well. *(LITTLE PRINCE sees that the AVIATOR has been sketching.)* Oh, yes. What a good idea.

AVIATOR. What?

THE LITTLE PRINCE – the play

LITTLE PRINCE. You could draw them. *(AVIATOR stops drawing.)* Then, for whoever looks at your pictures, it will be as if they made my journey as well.

AVIATOR. Wait a minute, I don't— *(Illustration J fades out.)*

LITTLE PRINCE. As I approached the next planet, it seemed to be inhabited by a very grand person. And he recognized me immediately as well.

(Music ends. ENSEMBLE puts LITTLE PRINCE down. They frame the scene as CONCEITED MAN enters. He is a ludicrous figure—a vaudevillian buffoon blissfully unaware of his ridiculousness.)

CONCEITED MAN. Ah! An admirer!

LITTLE PRINCE. Good morning. What a strange hat you're wearing.

CONCEITED MAN. It's a hat for acknowledging compliments. I raise it when people acclaim me. Unfortunately, nobody ever passes by this way. Now sit right down there. Very good—very good. Now slap your hands together—once again, now faster. *(LITTLE PRINCE claps and MAN raises his hat. They do this several times, accelerating until the clapping becomes applause to the CONCEITED MAN's delight.)* Ahh! Do you really admire me very much?

LITTLE PRINCE. Well, I—

CONCEITED MAN. I just love it when you—admire me.

LITTLE PRINCE. Admire—what does that mean?

CONCEITED MAN. It means you regard me as the handsomest, best-dressed, richest, most intelligent man on this planet.

LITTLE PRINCE & AVIATOR. But you are the *only* man on this planet.
CONCEITED MAN. Even so—couldn't you just admire me, anyway.

([Tape Cue #18] Lights crossfade to LITTLE PRINCE and AVIATOR, who is finishing up his drawing of the CONCEITED MAN by drawing his hat. Illustration K fades up.)

LITTLE PRINCE. I agreed to admire him, but I didn't know why that should be so important to him. *(Sees AVIATOR's drawing.)* Oh! That's very good.
AVIATOR. You think?
LITTLE PRINCE. I can almost see him tipping his hat.
AVIATOR. Grown-ups are very fond of hats.
LITTLE PRINCE. I know. I found them to be altogether very strange.
AVIATOR. So have I. Go on. What happened next? *(ENSEMBLE lifts LITTLE PRINCE into the stars. AVIATOR flips page of pad and follows as Illustration K fades out.)*
LITTLE PRINCE. There was so much I didn't understand. My flower—she cast her fragrance and radiance over me and I ought never to have left her. The next planet I visited belonged to a businessman who was so busy.

(The BUSINESSMAN, a caricature of a wheeler-dealer, has entered. ENSEMBLE lowers LITTLE PRINCE into scene, which they frame with their stars.)

BUSINESSMAN. Three and two make five. Five and seven make twelve.

THE LITTLE PRINCE – the play

LITTLE PRINCE. Good morning.
BUSINESSMAN. ...Twenty-six and five makes thirty-one. That makes five hundred-and-one million, six hundred twenty-two thousand, seven hundred thirty-one. *(Music ends.)*
LITTLE PRINCE. Five hundred million what?
BUSINESSMAN. I can't stop now. I'm much too busy. Can't you see? I'm concerned with important things. Five hundred million— *(Having lost count.)* Brmm!— Three and two make—
LITTLE PRINCE. Millions of what?
BUSINESSMAN *(exasperated)*. Millions of those little objects in the sky.
LITTLE PRINCE. Flies?
BUSINESSMAN. No, no. Glittering objects.
AVIATOR. Fireflies?
BUSINESSMAN. No! Little golden objects that set lazy men to idle dreaming.
LITTLE PRINCE. Ah! You mean the stars?
BUSINESSMAN. Yes, that's it, the stars. As for me, I am concerned with important things. No time for idle dreaming in my life.
LITTLE PRINCE. So you said. What do you do with five hundred millions of stars?
BUSINESSMAN. What do I do with— What do I do with them?
LITTLE PRINCE. Yes.
BUSINESSMAN. Nothing. I own them.
LITTLE PRINCE & AVIATOR. You own the stars?
BUSINESSMAN. Yes.
LITTLE PRINCE. But I have already seen a king who—

BUSINESSMAN. Kings do not *own*, they *reign over*. It's very different.
LITTLE PRINCE. How can anyone own the stars?
BUSINESSMAN. To whom do they belong?
LITTLE PRINCE. I don't know. To nobody.
BUSINESSMAN. They belong to me. Because I was the first person to think of it.
LITTLE PRINCE. What good does it do to own the stars?
BUSINESSMAN. It makes me rich.
LITTLE PRINCE. And what good does that do you?
BUSINESSMAN. I can put them in the bank.
LITTLE PRINCE. What does that mean?
BUSINESSMAN. It means I write down the number of my stars on a piece of paper, *[Tape Cue #19]* and I put the paper in a drawer and lock it with a key.
LITTLE PRINCE. Hmm. I myself own a flower which I water every day. So it's of some use to my flower that I own her. But you are of no use at all to the stars.

(BUSINESSMAN exits muttering. ENSEMBLE lifts LITTLE PRINCE and carry him around in a small circle.)

I traveled onward, and soon noticed a lonely flickering light.

(AVIATOR begins sketching. Illustration L fades up. ENSEMBLE stops and faces the drawing on the screen, with some of their stars framing the screen as the sketching continues. Focus is on the live drawing until music concludes.)

And there, on a planet even smaller than my own, stood a sweet old man dressed for a cold winter, faithfully lighting his street lamp.

THE LITTLE PRINCE – the play 33

(As Illustration L fades out, the LAMPLIGHTER appears with his lamp. ENSEMBLE lowers LITTLE PRINCE and frames the scene as before. [NOTE: Throughout the scene, the LAMPLIGHTER intermittently lights and extinguishes his street lamp with a long pole. Whenever he extinguishes his lamp, ENSEMBLE's "stars" must also simultaneously go out. If their stars are small lights, this can be done with an "on/off" switch on each branch. If their stars are cut-outs, they need to remove them from view in one short efficient movement. Likewise, when he lights his lamp, the stars must be turned on, or be returned to view.] The scene begins as the LAMPLIGHTER extinguishes his lamp.)

LITTLE PRINCE. Good morning! Why have you just put your lamp out?

LAMPLIGHTER. Those are the orders. G'morning.

LITTLE PRINCE. What are the orders?

LAMPLIGHTER. The orders are that I—oops— *(He lights it again.)* Good evening.

LITTLE PRINCE. But why have you just lighted it again?

LAMPLIGHTER. Those are the orders.

LITTLE PRINCE. I don't understand.

LAMPLIGHTER. There's nothing to understand. Orders are orders! I follow a terrible profession. In the old days, it was reasonable. I'd put the lamp out in the morning and in the evening I'd light it again. I had the rest of the day for relaxation and the rest of the night for sleep.

LITTLE PRINCE. The orders have changed since then?

LAMPLIGHTER *(extinguishes lamp)*. Good morning. The orders have NOT been changed. Now that's the tragedy. You see, year after year, the planet has turned faster and

faster. And the orders have not been changed. Now once every minute I have to light my lamp and put it out again.
LITTLE PRINCE *(laughs).* That's very funny. A day only lasts a minute here.
LAMPLIGHTER. It's not funny at all. *(LAMPLIGHTER lights lamp.)* Good evening. While we've been talking together a whole month has gone by.
LITTLE PRINCE & AVIATOR. A whole month?
LITTLE PRINCE. I could tell you a way you could rest whenever you want to...
LAMPLIGHTER. Oh, tell me, tell me. I always want to rest. *(He extinguishes his lamp.)* Good morning.
LITTLE PRINCE. Your planet is so small that three steps would take you all the way around. So all you would have to do is walk around slowly, very slowly, and the day will last as long as you like. I do it on my planet all the time to make the sunsets come.
LAMPLIGHTER. That doesn't do me much good, I'm afraid. If there's one thing I like to do in this life, it's sleep. And you can't sleep if you're walking. *(He lights the lamp.)* Good evening.
AVIATOR. Then you're unlucky.
LAMPLIGHTER. I am unlucky. Good morning... Good evening... *(LAMPLIGHTER begins to exit as he fades out of sight, [Tape Cue #20] continuing to mumble his salutation.)* Good morning... Good evening...

(ENSEMBLE's stars frame LITTLE PRINCE as he faces forward to speak to AVIATOR.)

LITTLE PRINCE. To me, that man was the only one who didn't seem selfish. Perhaps because he cared about his

THE LITTLE PRINCE – the play 35

work. What he did was useful, and therefore beautiful. Your drawing looks very much like him.
AVIATOR. Does it?
LITTLE PRINCE. He was the only one of them all I could have made my friend. *(ENSEMBLE whisks LITTLE PRINCE up, but they stand in place.)* But there was not enough room on his planet for two people. *(ENSEMBLE circles around quickly as LITTLE PRINCE speaks.)* The last planet I visited was that of...

(GEOGRAPHER enters as the lights come up on next planet. ENSEMBLE stops short, directly in front of him. He is an academician with a very upper-class British accent.)

GEOGRAPHER. A geographer. *(Pronounced "jographuh." ENSEMBLE lowers LITTLE PRINCE and resumes their framing position.)*
LITTLE PRINCE. What is a jographuh?
GEOGRAPHER. A geographer is a scholar who knows the locations of all the seas, rivers, towns, mountains and deserts.
LITTLE PRINCE. That's very interesting. Your planet is beautiful. Does it have any oceans?
GEOGRAPHER. I couldn't tell you.
LITTLE PRINCE. Ah. Has it any mountains?
GEOGRAPHER. Don't know.
LITTLE PRINCE. What about towns, rivers and deserts? *(The GEOGRAPHER shakes his head.)*
AVIATOR. But you're a jographuh!
GEOGRAPHER. Exactly. But I am *not* an explorer. Explorers count the towns, rivers, mountains, seas, oceans

and deserts. Geographers are much too important to do that. We stay at our desks and record what the explorers recall of their travels. *(Music ends.)* Why, I recognize you now—*you're* an explorer! You can describe my planet to me. No. Wait. You come from far away. Describe *your* planet to me.

LITTLE PRINCE. Well... I have a flower. She's the most beautiful thing on my planet.

GEOGRAPHER. We don't record flowers.

LITTLE PRINCE. Why not?

GEOGRAPHER. Because they are ephemeral.

LITTLE PRINCE. What does that mean—ephemeral?

GEOGRAPHER. It means "in danger of speedy disappearance."

AVIATOR *(reflectively)*. In danger of speedy disappearance...

LITTLE PRINCE. My flower is in danger of speedy disappearance?

GEOGRAPHER. Certainly it is.

LITTLE PRINCE. My flower is ephemeral, and she has only four thorns to defend herself against the world and I have left her on my planet all alone! What do I do?

GEOGRAPHER. Why don't you visit the planet Earth? I hear it has a good reputation.

(LITTLE PRINCE turns to audience. ENSEMBLE's stars gather around him obscuring the GEOGRAPHER's exit. In the peripheral darkness, AVIATOR exits and SNAKE enters behind ENSEMBLE.)

LITTLE PRINCE. So I did. As soon as I arrived, here on Earth, I met someone...

THE LITTLE PRINCE – the play 37

([Tape Cue #21] The stars peel away and exit in different directions, revealing the SNAKE. She is seductive, and understands her great power.)

LITTLE PRINCE. Good evening.
SNAKE. Good evening.
LITTLE PRINCE. What planet is this?
SNAKE. This is Earth. This is Africa.
LITTLE PRINCE. Ah, then there are no people on Earth?
SNAKE. This is the desert. There are no people in the desert. The Earth is large.
LITTLE PRINCE *(looks toward his star)*. Look at my planet. It's right there above us.
SNAKE. It's very beautiful.
LITTLE PRINCE. I wonder whether the stars shine brightly here so that each of us can find his way home.
SNAKE. What has brought you here?
LITTLE PRINCE. I have been having some trouble with a flower.
SNAKE. A flower. Ah! *(Her snake-like movements have a hypnotic effect on LITTLE PRINCE from which he ultimately extricates himself.)*
LITTLE PRINCE. Where are the men? It is very lonely in the desert.
SNAKE. It is also lonely—among men.
LITTLE PRINCE. You are a funny animal! You are no thicker than a finger.
SNAKE. But I am more powerful than the finger of a king.
LITTLE PRINCE. You're not very powerful. You don't have any feet.
SNAKE. But I can carry you further than any ship. Whomever I touch I send back to the earth from whence they

came. But you, you are innocent and true and come from a star. You move me to pity. You are so weak on this Earth made of granite. I can help you some day. If you grow too homesick, I can— I CAN. *(She moves menacingly around him, finally confronting him.)* Do you know who I am?
LITTLE PRINCE. Oh yes, very well.

(Music ends. On final beat, lights cut from pose of LITTLE PRINCE and SNAKE to drawing of LITTLE PRINCE in the same position on projection screen. See Illustration M. Lights come up slowly on AVIATOR alone on stage, staring intently at his pad and drawing. It is night. [Tape Cue #22] Snake music is heard. SNAKE suddenly appears behind him looking over his shoulder at drawing.)

AVIATOR. You shouldn't be talking to snakes, you know. *(He adds the SNAKE to the drawing.)* They're dangerous. And you certainly shouldn't trust them. They're treacherous creatures. *(AVIATOR continues to draw, unaware of SNAKE.)*
SNAKE *(seeing AVIATOR's drawing)*. That's very good.

(AVIATOR looks up in shock. Illustration M goes off.)

You've been hiding your talent.

(AVIATOR moves away. Throughout the following, SNAKE continues to move with serpent-like movements punctuating her speech.)

AVIATOR. What's going on here?

THE LITTLE PRINCE – the play

SNAKE. You shouldn't tell him not to trust me. I never lie. It's all a matter of perception. Lies—truth, snakes—hats, death—life... What appears to be is not always what is. But then you know that—or do you anymore? He knows who I am. Do you?

(SNAKE rattle is heard as she vanishes. AVIATOR is in shock, alone. Lights change. The AVIATOR works frantically on his plane.)

AVIATOR *(to audience)*. Understandably, I was upset. Not only were my food and water nearly gone, but now I was having serious hallucinations. I worked frantically through the night and the next day, determined to make my plane work. I was at my wit's end when, at sunset, of course—

(LITTLE PRINCE enters and speaks with urgency.)

LITTLE PRINCE. Please, I have to know, you have to tell me— *(AVIATOR bangs away at the plane.)* It's very important. I have to know— If sheep eat little bushes, do they eat flowers, too? *(AVIATOR continues working.)* Please. *(AVIATOR glances at him but continues working.)* Will it eat my flower?
AVIATOR *(not stopping)*. Yes—sheep will eat anything.
LITTLE PRINCE. Even flowers that have thorns?
AVIATOR *(stops banging, goes to radio)*. Even flowers that have thorns.
LITTLE PRINCE. Then why do they have them?

| AVIATOR *(tries radio)*. Come in— Come in Tangiers— Morocco— Cairo— Anybody! | LITTLE PRINCE. What good are they? If they don't protect them. Why? |

AVIATOR *(angrily)*. Flowers have thorns just for spite. *(Slams down radio.)*

LITTLE PRINCE. I don't believe you! Flowers are naive creatures. They would never act out of spite. If they hurt you, it's because they don't understand. And you actually believe that the flowers—

AVIATOR. No no no! I don't believe anything! I just said the first thing that came into my head. Can't you see I'm busy with important things here?

LITTLE PRINCE. Important things? You talk just like the grown-ups.

AVIATOR. The grown-ups. I'm not—

LITTLE PRINCE. You mix everything up together... you confuse everything. I don't believe you could ever be an artist!

AVIATOR. An artist? Being an artist is not going to get me out of here! This is a matter of life and death—don't you understand? Do you know how much time I've wasted on pictures of your silly stories?! *(He throws the drawings and they scatter. Music ends. A sudden silence. LITTLE PRINCE is stunned; AVIATOR is embarrassed.)*

LITTLE PRINCE *(solemnly)*. You are like the Businessman.

AVIATOR. The Businessman? Wait, I—

LITTLE PRINCE. He has never smelled a flower. He has never looked at a star. He has never loved anyone. *(He*

THE LITTLE PRINCE – the play

begins to get upset.) And all day he says over and over, just like you: "I am busy with important things." But he is not a man, he's—a mushroom!

AVIATOR. I—

LITTLE PRINCE *(with mounting distress).* The flowers have been growing thorns for millions of years. For millions of years, the sheep have been eating them just the same. And it's not important to try to understand why the flowers go to so much trouble to grow thorns which are of no use to them?

AVIATOR. Little man, please, I—

LITTLE PRINCE *(fighting off tears).* And I know— I myself—know one flower which is unique in all the world, but which one sheep can destroy in a single bite some morning without even noticing what he's doing. You think that's not IMPORTANT? *(He starts to cry. [Tape Cue #23].)*

AVIATOR. Please—please... I'm sorry... The flower that you love is not in danger. I'll draw you a muzzle for your sheep. I'll draw you a railing to put around your flower— *(AVIATOR touches LITTLE PRINCE. LITTLE PRINCE pulls away. They stare at each other for a moment. Music ends. LITTLE PRINCE runs off.)* I'll... *(AVIATOR slowly gathers up the drawings he had scattered. He looks toward where LITTLE PRINCE exited.)* A grown-up. So that's what I am. One of them... Have you gone just because the stars have come out? Or are you never coming back again? I wouldn't blame you if you didn't... *(To audience.)* I didn't know what to say. How to reach him. How I could ever mend the damage I had done. Then I had an idea.

(Screen comes up. He draws a muzzle. See Illustration N. He offers it out to where LITTLE PRINCE had been.)

It's a muzzle for your sheep so you never need worry about your flower anymore. *(To audience again.)* But he, of course, was too far away to hear. It's such a secret place—the land of tears.

*(The AVIATOR walks despondently to his plane. **[Tape Cue #24]** The sound of the SNAKE grows slowly until it becomes a jolting rattle as light reveals the silhouette of SNAKE, standing and writhing in a menacing pose. AVIATOR does not see her, but hears the rattle and decides to run after LITTLE PRINCE. He quickly grabs his canteen and all the scattered drawings and runs out.)*

Wait, wait...

OPTIONAL INTERMISSION

*(**[Tape Cue #25]** Lights come up on LITTLE PRINCE sitting on dune facing U watching a yellow sunset. This is created [as in Act One] by the central glow of the stage lights, embellished by the ENSEMBLE's waving of shards of fabric from the stage wings on each side. AVIATOR runs in, stops when he sees LITTLE PRINCE. AVIATOR is carrying his knapsack and holding the drawing of the muzzle.)*

AVIATOR *(to audience)*. I had searched the desert through the night and all the next day and, as usual, I didn't see him until— *(ENSEMBLE suddenly changes the color of the sunset to orange as the stage lights change likewise. To LITTLE PRINCE.)* So far away from home, it's good to

THE LITTLE PRINCE – the play

have someone to watch the sunset with. *(LITTLE PRINCE does not respond. The sunset ends with the sunset music. As the music changes, the starry night sky fades up. AVIATOR sits facing audience as he makes an attempt at an apology.)* Once I saw a beautiful house made of rosy-colored brick, with geraniums in the window and doves on the roof. And I thought of telling someone about it, but I knew that from that description they would never be able to appreciate it. If, on the other hand, I were to say, "I saw a house that costs a million dollars," they would say, "Oh, what a beautiful house that must be." *(LITTLE PRINCE laughs. AVIATOR is encouraged and turns toward him.)* You see, I realized last night that I have become like those people. So, sometimes, when you talk to me about things, I can't quite appreciate how important they are to you. *(AVIATOR turns away.)* I can't see sheep through walls of boxes anymore.

LITTLE PRINCE *(finally turns toward AVIATOR and notices the drawing).* What is that? *(AVIATOR looks up.)* It looks very complicated.

AVIATOR *(realizes what he's referring to and goes to him).* Oh, it's a muzzle—for your sheep. So you don't have to worry about his eating your flower. *(LITTLE PRINCE does not understand.)* You put it on him like this. *(AVIATOR tries to mime a sheep with a muzzle on. LITTLE PRINCE smiles.)*

LITTLE PRINCE. I see. How is your friend?

AVIATOR. Oh, him. No change, I'm afraid.

LITTLE PRINCE. He'll be better soon. I'm sure of it. After I landed here, nearly a year ago now, I traveled many places... *(Music ends.)*

44 THE LITTLE PRINCE – the play

AVIATOR. Oh yes. Would you tell me about them? *(To audience.)* And so, he continued to tell me stories, and though my circumstances were more dire than ever, I stopped, and I listened— *(AVIATOR gets his pad.)* — and I drew.

([Tape Cue #26] [NOTE: In this sequence, the stage lights and/or the ENSEMBLE will make a series of sunsets—each sunset on a different day, accompanying that day's story: orange for the Desert Flower story, purple for the Mountain Echo story, and red for the Wall of Roses story. Each sunset should change on the musical cue which begins each story.] Lights change. Orange sunset begins. AVIATOR draws the Desert Flower [Illustration O] as it is drawn on the projection screen. The DESERT FLOWER can be an offstage voice or an onstage actor. When speaking to her, LITTLE PRINCE addresses the screen or the person, as the case may be.)

LITTLE PRINCE. After I met the snake, I crossed the desert and met a single flower. A flower of no importance at all. Good morning.
DESERT FLOWER. Good morning.
LITTLE PRINCE. Where are the men?
DESERT FLOWER. Men? I think there are six or seven of them in existence. I saw them several years ago passing by. But one never knows where to find them. The wind blows them away. They have no roots and that makes their lives very difficult.
LITTLE PRINCE. I see. Goodbye.
DESERT FLOWER. Goodbye. *(Illustration O fades out. Purple sunset begins.)*

THE LITTLE PRINCE – the play

LITTLE PRINCE. After that,

(Illustration P comes up.)

I climbed a high mountain. From a mountain this high, I thought I would surely be able to see your whole planet and all the people on it. But I saw nothing but peaks of rock that were sharp like needles. Good morning.

(MOUNTAIN ECHO VOICES are offstage from various parts of stage.)

MOUNTAIN ECHO. Good morning— Good morning— Good morning—
LITTLE PRINCE. Who are you?
MOUNTAIN ECHO. Who are you— Who are you— Who are you?
LITTLE PRINCE. Be my friend. I am all alone.
MOUNTAIN ECHO. I am all alone—all alone—all alone.
LITTLE PRINCE. This planet is so strange. The people here have no imagination. They repeat whatever you say to them. *(Illustration P fades out.)* On my planet I have— I used to have—a flower. She was always the first to speak... Finally,

(Red sunset begins. Illustration Q comes up.)

after walking for a long time through sand and rocks and snow, I came upon a road that led to a garden

(As Illustration Q fades, lights come up on ENSEMBLE holding large red papier-mâché roses at varying heights,

forming a WALL OF ROSES. You can create an even larger wall by using up to twelve additional people, as noted in the cast list.)

with an entire wall of flowers. *(ROSES giggle.)* Good morning.

WALL OF ROSES *(giggling)*. Good morning.
LITTLE PRINCE *(approaches WALL OF ROSES)*. As I came closer, I saw—they all looked like my flower! Who are you?
WALL OF ROSES *(giggling)*. We are roses.
LITTLE PRINCE. But I thought my flower was the only one of her kind in the whole universe. I thought I was rich with a flower that was unique in all the world. And all I had was a common rose. A common rose.

(LITTLE PRINCE lies down and cries as lights come down and focus on him. WALL OF ROSES exits and ENSEMBLE reenters as trees. They face U in various tree-like positions, holding the multibranched sticks, this time dotted with leaves instead of stars. The trees are scattered around the stage like a grove so that the FOX can use them to scamper between and hide behind. Drawing of FOX comes up. Artist adds apple to it. One prominent tree then displays an apple. See Illustration R.)

FOX. Good morning.
LITTLE PRINCE *(stops crying, looks around)*. Good morning.
FOX *(scampers across to a tree)*. I'm right here under the apple tree.

THE LITTLE PRINCE – the play 47

LITTLE PRINCE. Who are you? You're very pretty to look at. *(LITTLE PRINCE starts to approach FOX. FOX scampers away nervously. Music ends.)*

FOX. I'm a fox.

LITTLE PRINCE. Will you come play with me? I'm so unhappy. *(Illustration R fades out. LITTLE PRINCE moves toward him. FOX growls.)*

FOX. Play with you— I can't play with you!

LITTLE PRINCE. Why not?

FOX. Because—because— I'm not tamed—and you're a— one of them.

LITTLE PRINCE. Them? *([Tape Cue #27] FOX scampers away again.)*

FOX. The ones...with the guns. The hunters. *(FOX scampers nervously.)* Yeah, you're one of those hunters...oh, sure, you don't look dangerous cause you're little. But how can I be sure it's not a trap. Very clever. No, No, as things are, I'd better just— *(FOX begins to scamper off. LITTLE PRINCE stops FOX from leaving as music ends.)*

LITTLE PRINCE. But I don't have a gun! *(FOX stops and looks as LITTLE PRINCE opens his arms wide to display no concealed weapon.)* See.

FOX *(looking around).* Then you'd better watch out for them, too. *(He keeps his distance throughout the scene.)*

LITTLE PRINCE. What does that mean "tamed"?

FOX. You don't live around here, do you?

LITTLE PRINCE. What does that mean "tamed"?

FOX. What are you looking for?

LITTLE PRINCE. I was looking for men.

FOX. Men— Brrr! Grr. They have guns and they hunt. It's very disturbing!

LITTLE PRINCE. Oh.

FOX. They also raise chickens. Guns and chickens. These are their only interests.
LITTLE PRINCE. Ah.
FOX. Are you looking for chickens?
LITTLE PRINCE. What?
FOX. Chickens.
LITTLE PRINCE. No. I was looking for men.
FOX. Oh, that's right.
LITTLE PRINCE. What does that mean "tamed"?
FOX *(sighs)*. Boy, you don't let go of a question, do you? It's an act too often neglected. It means...to establish ties.
LITTLE PRINCE. To establish ties?
FOX. Yeah...see, to me you're just another little boy just like a hundred thousand other little boys and I have no need of you. And you—well, have no need of me. To you, I'm nothing more than a fox like a hundred thousand other foxes.
LITTLE PRINCE. Oh, I see.
FOX. But if you tamed me—to me you'd be unique in all the world. And to you, I'd be unique in all the world. Then—we'd need each other.
LITTLE PRINCE. I'm beginning to understand. There was a flower—a rose.
FOX. Like the ones on that wall down the road?
LITTLE PRINCE *(nods sadly)*. I think she tried to tame me.
FOX. It's possible. On Earth one sees all sorts of things.
LITTLE PRINCE. Oh, but this wasn't on Earth.
FOX. Wasn't on Earth?
LITTLE PRINCE. No.
FOX. Some other planet, maybe?
LITTLE PRINCE. Yes.
FOX. Right—are there hunters on that planet?

THE LITTLE PRINCE – the play 49

LITTLE PRINCE. No.
FOX. Hmm... Are there chickens?
LITTLE PRINCE. No.
FOX. Well, nothing's perfect.
LITTLE PRINCE. No.
FOX. No. *(Pause.)* My life, you know...it's, well, it's... I hunt chickens. Men hunt me. All the chickens are alike. All the men are alike. It's—very monotonous.
LITTLE PRINCE. What?
FOX. Well see, I search me out a chicken—hey, a fella's got to eat. But then, the hunters, they chase me through the woods and down the hills until I have to dive into a hole to hide from them until they give up. Ev'ry day it's pretty much the same old thing *(Yawn.)* Search, run, hide. Sometimes I sit down in that hole for hours just thinking.
LITTLE PRINCE. About what?
FOX. About—what it might be like if it was—different. If someday, someone came along—someone without a gun. Someone whose footsteps would make me excited instead of sending me scurrying away. Someone who would— *(He looks at LITTLE PRINCE.)* ...tame me.
LITTLE PRINCE. I'd like to, really, but I don't have much time. I have so many things to understand.
FOX. You only understand the things you tame. Men have no time to understand anything, so they have no friends. If you want to understand—if you want a friend—you've got to tame me.
LITTLE PRINCE. What must I do to tame you?
FOX. You must be very patient. I'm still a wild animal, after all. First, we'll sit down together in the grass. *(FOX indicates LITTLE PRINCE to sit further and further away*

until they are quite far apart.) Then I'll look at you out of the corner of my eye and you will say nothing. Words are the source of misunderstanding. But everyday we will sit a little closer. Day after day.

LITTLE PRINCE. Shall we begin?
FOX. Tomorrow. Meet me right here.
LITTLE PRINCE. Tomorrow?
FOX. Tomorrow.

(LITTLE PRINCE exits. Lights change. LITTLE PRINCE reenters.)

LITTLE PRINCE. Good morning! *(LITTLE PRINCE catches FOX asleep and is much too close. FOX reflexively growls ferociously and snaps, catching LITTLE PRINCE's hand in his mouth. After a moment he slowly extracts it, battling with his own nature. LITTLE PRINCE rubs his hand. FOX puts distance between them.)*
FOX. Say—uh— Don't *do* that!
LITTLE PRINCE. What is it that—
FOX. Like I said, my experience with people has not been all that good. You okay there?
LITTLE PRINCE. I think so.
FOX. You know, maybe this just isn't such a good idea, maybe—
LITTLE PRINCE. No, no really, I'm fine. But—what is it that I did?
FOX. WELL! You can't just stroll up for a visit anytime at all. If you're gonna tame me, you've got to come at the same time every day. Didn't I mention that? *(LITTLE PRINCE shakes his head.)* It's got to be a ritual. If you come at the same time every day, then every day about

THE LITTLE PRINCE – the play

an hour before you're due, I'll start getting excited. Rituals are very important. Especially in taming.
LITTLE PRINCE. I think I understand.
FOX. Do you think? You see those grain fields down yonder. Well, wheat is of no use to me. I mean, the wheatfields have nothing to say to me and that is sad. But you have hair that is the color of gold. Now if you tamed me, the wheat, which is also golden, will bring me back the thought of you and I shall love to listen to the wind in the wheat.
LITTLE PRINCE. I understand now. Shall we begin?
FOX. Ready when you are.
BOTH. One, two, three, go!

([Tape Cue #28] They proceed to perform a ritual representing the taming process. As the clock ticks, they start from DC and move in opposite directions toward the wings, saluting each other as they go. They circle around U through the trees and then back D, passing the point where they started. They come to rest at a distance from each other on the D proscenium. The lights indicate the passage of a day (i.e. they dim to their darkest when the actors are U and return to their brightest as the actors reach their new positions. LITTLE PRINCE and FOX face the audience, occasionally looking at each other out of the corner of their eyes, awkwardly trying to maintain a silence. [NOTE: During the tick-tock metronome sound of the music, the ENSEMBLE's trees may add to the fun by tilting their heads from side to side in half time. When LITTLE PRINCE and FOX speak, the trees should freeze.])

LITTLE PRINCE. I was thinking, did you ever—
FOX. Shh. Not a word! *(Disappointed at their failure, they repeat circle action, saluting as they go, with lighting changes, [NOTE: When the ritual begins again, ENSEMBLE's trees could add a light bouncing at the knees to their head-tilting. When LITTLE PRINCE and FOX speak, the trees freeze.] This time they arrive a little closer to one another. Again they stand facing the audience in awkward silence.)* Nice scarf.
LITTLE PRINCE. Nice tail.
FOX. It was a gift from my mother.

(Repeat same actions, saluting again, circling more hopefully. Their movements accelerate as music builds. They extend their pattern to make a figure-8 past each other. Then they do-si-do around each other. [NOTE: This time, ENSEMBLE's trees not only bob heads, and bounce at knees, but they also move their branches gently from side to side. Ultimately, they mirror the figure-8 and do-si-do patterns being made by LITTLE PRINCE and FOX. As the music peaks, they have do-si-doed themselves right off the stage. LITTLE PRINCE and FOX finally arrive face to face.)

LITTLE PRINCE. Are you tame now?
FOX. I don't know. Let's find out. *(Slowly LITTLE PRINCE reaches to touch him. FOX tries to fight off urge to growl and finally LITTLE PRINCE pets him. FOX doesn't growl. In fact, much to his surprise, he nuzzles LITTLE PRINCE.)* YES! I'm tame! I'm finally tame. *(They sit. FOX nuzzles like a puppy dog as lights fade.)*

THE LITTLE PRINCE – the play 53

(Tape cue ends. After a brief pause, lights come up. LITTLE PRINCE is sitting, absorbed in his own thoughts as the FOX is moving around playfully.)

FOX. Let's see. Yesterday we explored the hills, and the day before, the forest. Shall we dance today, or shall we chase each other through the wheatfields?
LITTLE PRINCE. No. I don't think so. *(LITTLE PRINCE sits down in the grass.)*
FOX. I know. Let's play hide and seek. I'll hide. I've had lots of practice.
LITTLE PRINCE. Not today.
FOX *(nestles down next to him. After a moment:)*. You are thinking about your Rose again. Listen to me. Go now and take another look at the wall full of roses and you'll understand.
LITTLE PRINCE. Understand what?
FOX. You'll see. Then come back to say goodbye to me.
LITTLE PRINCE. Goodbye? What do you mean?
FOX. Just go. And when you come back I will tell you a secret.

(As LITTLE PRINCE returns to the WALL OF ROSES, they are giggling. He sees them with greater understanding and sighs.)

LITTLE PRINCE. You are not at all like my rose. As yet you are nothing. No one has tamed you, and you have tamed no one. You are beautiful, but you are empty. One could not die for you. You are like my fox when I first met him—like a hundred thousand other foxes. But now I have tamed him, and made him my friend and now he is unique in all the world. An ordinary passerby would think that my rose looked just like you—the rose that belongs to me. But she is more important than all the hundreds of you other *[Tape Cue #29]* roses because it is *she* that I have watered; because it is *she* that I have sheltered behind the screen; because it is for *her* that I have killed the caterpillars except the two or three we saved to become butterflies, because it is *she* that I have listened to when she asked questions, or grumbled, or even sometimes when she said nothing, because she is *my* rose.

(ROSE appears through the scrim. Now she is surrounded by several of the ENSEMBLE's menacing baobabs, now grown to elbow length. ROSE and LITTLE PRINCE reach toward each other. ROSE disappears. Music changes. LITTLE PRINCE returns to FOX.)

LITTLE PRINCE. The time has come for me to go.
FOX. Ah... I shall cry.
LITTLE PRINCE. But I never wished you harm—you wanted me to tame you.
FOX. Yes, that is so.
LITTLE PRINCE. Then it has done you no good at all.
FOX. It has done me good—because of the wheatfields. I will always remember you when I see them because they are the color of your hair. One runs the risk of weeping a little, when one allows himself to be tamed.
LITTLE PRINCE. Goodbye.
FOX. Goodbye. And now here is my secret. A very simple secret. Repeat after me so you will always remember it. It is only with the heart that one can see rightly. *(FOX lays his hand on LITTLE PRINCE's heart.)*

THE LITTLE PRINCE – the play

LITTLE PRINCE. It is only with the heart that one can see rightly. *(LITTLE PRINCE lays his hand on FOX's heart.)*
FOX. What is essential is invisible to the eye. *(FOX touches LITTLE PRINCE's eye.)*
LITTLE PRINCE. What is essential is invisible to the eye.

(LITTLE PRINCE touches FOX's eye. As FOX exits, they salute each other sadly. Music ends as lights cross to AVIATOR in desert who suddenly lets out a desperate wail as he holds empty canteen upside down realizing it is empty.)

AVIATOR. Nooo!
LITTLE PRINCE. What is it? What—
AVIATOR. These memories of yours are very charming but—
LITTLE PRINCE. But what?
AVIATOR. But my plane is still not working and— *(AVIATOR tips his canteen upside down.)* I don't have another drop of water to drink.
LITTLE PRINCE. My friend the Fox—
AVIATOR. This really is no longer a matter that has anything to do with your fox.
LITTLE PRINCE. Why not?
AVIATOR. Because I am about to die of thirst. Not that there is anything I can do about it. And I suppose there are worse ways to die than listening to your stories.
LITTLE PRINCE. It's a good thing to have had a friend even if one is about to die. I'm thirsty, too. Come. Let's look for a well. *(Turns, begins to walk.)*
AVIATOR. In the desert?

([Tape Cue #30] LITTLE PRINCE looks back. He is already on his way. AVIATOR shrugs—and follows. They are seen walking in various stretches of the desert.)

LITTLE PRINCE. One never ought to listen to flowers. One should simply look at them and breathe their fragrance. Mine perfumed all my planet, but I didn't know how to take pleasure in all her grace. *(They stop.)* I should have guessed all the affection behind her silly little games.

(Music continues. LITTLE PRINCE resumes walking. AVIATOR follows. They are seen elsewhere.)

LITTLE PRINCE. The men where you live raise five thousand roses in the same garden—and they don't find what they're looking for. *(They stop.)* And yet what they're looking for could be found in one single rose...or a little water. *(LITTLE PRINCE moves on.)*
AVIATOR. A little water.

(AVIATOR follows. Music continues. They arrive at another place. The stars have come out. AVIATOR stumbles with exhaustion and falls.)

LITTLE PRINCE. I'm tired. Let's rest for a moment. *(Music ends.)*
AVIATOR. In all the time we've been together I've never seen you take a single drink of water and yet you did say before that you were thirsty, didn't you? Didn't you?
LITTLE PRINCE. Water may also be good for the heart. *(AVIATOR does not understand. LITTLE PRINCE looks*

THE LITTLE PRINCE – the play

at stars.) The stars are beautiful because of a flower that cannot be seen.

AVIATOR. Yes, I suppose so.

LITTLE PRINCE. The desert is beautiful, too. What makes the desert beautiful is that somewhere it hides a well.

AVIATOR. Do you really think we'll find a well in the desert?

LITTLE PRINCE. You must remember my fox's secret. *[Tape Cue #31]* It is only with the heart that one can see rightly. What is essential is invisible to the eye.

(LITTLE PRINCE has repeated the FOX's hand gestures. LITTLE PRINCE goes to sleep. AVIATOR stares out. With his last bit of energy he draws two dunes and a star. See Illustration S.)

AVIATOR. Are you really hiding a well?

([Tape Cue #32] Chimes are heard. AVIATOR turns toward LITTLE PRINCE with new understanding. Illustration S fades out. AVIATOR approaches LITTLE PRINCE and gently picks him up, cradles him in his arms, faces audience, and speaks, as lights come down to a spot on him.)

AVIATOR. I took him in my arms and set out walking once more. It seemed to me that I was carrying a very fragile treasure. To me it seemed that there was nothing more fragile on all the Earth. In the moonlight I looked at his pale forehead, his closed eyes, his locks of hair that trembled in the wind, and I said to myself, "What I see here is nothing but a shell. What is most important is invisible." What moved me so deeply about this little man—this little prince*—was his loyalty to a flower—the image of a rose that shone through his whole being like the flame of a lamp, even while he slept. And I felt him to be more fragile still. As if he himself were a flame that might be extinguished by a little puff of wind.

(As music continues with the female voices singing, AVIATOR, exhausted and desperate, carries LITTLE PRINCE through the "dunes." [NOTE: In the dark during AVIATOR's speech, ENSEMBLE has placed across the length of the stage, wing to wing, two 4-foot wide lengths of sand-colored nylon (parachute fabric or other lightweight fabric). These are parallel, but far enough apart, to allow AVIATOR carrying LITTLE PRINCE to cross the stage (U between the two fabrics) and then cross back again (U of them both). ENSEMBLE members, while standing, hold each length of fabric at both ends and create a traveling wave in slow motion. The illusion should be that of wind-blown dunes—an ever-changing sandy landscape in the moonlight. To assure this effect, the team holding the first fabric should begin their wave from L; the team holding the second fabric should begin 1-2 seconds later from R. Then the process is reversed and repeated throughout the music.] As the main theme of the music returns, in the dark, the well is put into place, either on a wagon or by ENSEMBLE members. Illustration T goes out.)

I carried him until I could not take another step. And then just as he'd said, out of nowhere, like a miracle...

---

* Cue for Illustration T.

THE LITTLE PRINCE – the play

(The lights have been changing from moonlight to dawn. On the words "out of nowhere," the lengths of each fabric, while in mid-air, should be released from one end and pulled offstage—one from R, one from L, revealing the well. AVIATOR sees the well.) Look! *(AVIATOR puts LITTLE PRINCE down. Desperately, they approach it and raise a bucket of water. AVIATOR gives him a drink and then drinks himself.)*

LITTLE PRINCE. Listen! Do you hear? We've awakened the well. It's singing. *(They drink companionably and laugh with relief. They play silly games like leapfrog and splash each other. Finally, the AVIATOR sighs and sits.)* What's the matter?

AVIATOR. Nothing, nothing at all. This is unbelievable. It's just so amazing. It's like I've been reborn just when I thought I was about to die. And you—you're responsible for this—for this change in me. You brought me here. You took me on this incredible journey. You.

LITTLE PRINCE. But you're wrong.

AVIATOR. What do you mean?

LITTLE PRINCE. It was *you* who walked all night through the desert. *You* who carried *me*. It was *you* who found the well.

AVIATOR. Amazing.

LITTLE PRINCE. It's not really. I knew from the moment you showed me your drawing of my sheep in a box that all you needed was some time—and a friend. And look at you now—you're tame.

AVIATOR *(in disbelief)*. Tame? *(Amused.)* Like your fox?

LITTLE PRINCE. Exactly... Like my fox.

(AVIATOR begins to laugh. LITTLE PRINCE joins him. This turns into riotous laughter during which LITTLE PRINCE pulls AVIATOR up off the ground. This turns into a brief game of "motor boat"—spinning around. AVIATOR then picks LITTLE PRINCE up, stretching him above his head and turning around ultimately landing him on his shoulders. Suddenly there is a beautiful multicolored sunset created by ENSEMBLE and the stage lighting. They stop and look, VOICES are heard.)

AVIATOR. I hear it! I hear it!

(Music fades out as AVIATOR puts LITTLE PRINCE down and stares in wonder at the sunset. LITTLE PRINCE watches him for a moment and smiles, then walks away a bit. His mood has changed. He is staring off very seriously. AVIATOR notices LITTLE PRINCE.)

What is it? What's going on in that amazing little mind of yours now? Do you want me to draw you another sheep to keep the one in the box company?

LITTLE PRINCE. No. One sheep is sufficient. He can eat the baobabs while I give my rose the attention she requires.

AVIATOR. I see.

LITTLE PRINCE. My descent to Earth—tonight will be its anniversary. I came down very near here.

AVIATOR. Then, that morning when I first met you—two weeks ago—when you were strolling along, all alone, a thousand miles from anywhere, then it wasn't by chance? You were on your way back to the place where you

THE LITTLE PRINCE – the play 61

landed? *(No answer.)* Perhaps it was because of the anniversary? *(No answer.)* You have plans I don't know about.
LITTLE PRINCE. You must go now and fix your friend.
AVIATOR. My friend? *You* are my friend.
LITTLE PRINCE. Go now. I will be waiting for you here. Come back in the evening.

(AVIATOR reluctantly returns to his plane. LITTLE PRINCE exits.)

AVIATOR. When I returned to my plane, unbelievable as it seems, as though there had never been anything wrong *[Tape Cue #33]* —it started. The engine revved and the propeller spun like a top. I was so excited. I had to tell my friend the good news. So I ran back ahead of time, but when I found him...he was deep in conversation.

(AVIATOR approaches LITTLE PRINCE who is talking to SNAKE. Tape cue continues.)

LITTLE PRINCE. Then you don't remember. This is not the exact spot. Yes, yes. It is the right day, but this is not the place. It's under my star where we met. Exactly. You will see my tracks in the sand. I shall be there tonight. You have good poison? You're sure it won't make me suffer too long? Now go away. I want to get down.

(On final chord of music, SNAKE directs a sharp look toward AVIATOR, then exits. Music ends.)

AVIATOR. What are you doing? Why are you talking with the snake?
LITTLE PRINCE. I'm glad your friend is better. Now you can go back home.
AVIATOR. How did you know about that?
LITTLE PRINCE. I too am going back home today. Back to my rose. It is much farther—much more difficult. I have your sheep and I have your sheep's box. And I have the muzzle.
AVIATOR. Little man, you're afraid.
LITTLE PRINCE. I shall be much more afraid tonight.
AVIATOR. You can't mean this. Tell me this is a bad dream—the snake, the meeting place, the star...
LITTLE PRINCE. The thing that is important is the thing that is invisible. Like a flower on a star.
AVIATOR. Yes, I know—
LITTLE PRINCE. Like a well in the desert.
AVIATOR. Yes.
LITTLE PRINCE. Like an elephant in a boa constrictor. I knew from the moment I saw you asleep by your machine, looking more like a child than any grown-up I ever knew. I knew that you could give me what I needed.
AVIATOR. And what was that? What have I given you?
LITTLE PRINCE. My sheep, of course. You drew me a sheep in a box. *(AVIATOR is almost crying.)* Please don't cry.
AVIATOR. One runs the risk of weeping, when one allows himself to be tamed. Oh, please don't, don't—do this. I want you to stay, I need you to stay. If you're gone—who will laugh for me?
LITTLE PRINCE. Just because I'm gone, doesn't mean I've gone away.
AVIATOR. What?

THE LITTLE PRINCE – the play

([Tape Cue #34] ENSEMBLE member appears (?) ing high a single star on a long pole. AVIATOR does(?) understand. LITTLE PRINCE points to the sky.)

LITTLE PRINCE. Do you see my star up there?
AVIATOR. Which one? There are so many.
LITTLE PRINCE. Maybe that's just as well. Then all the stars will be your friends.
AVIATOR. What do you mean?
LITTLE PRINCE. Each night, watch the sun set and see the stars come out. And know that *I* am there on one of them—living...and laughing. Then all the stars will laugh for you. *(LITTLE PRINCE stares at his star. The star appears to emanate a glowing shaft of light down on him.)* Please do not come tonight. It will look a little as if I were dying. That is not true. It's just that this body is too heavy for me to carry all that way. The snake is just providing me with transportation. Don't be sad. What will be left will be nothing but an old empty shell. There's nothing sad about empty shells, is there?

(AVIATOR embraces LITTLE PRINCE. Music continues. Snake rattle is heard as SNAKE appears, awaiting LITTLE PRINCE.)

LITTLE PRINCE. You must not stay now.
AVIATOR. I will not leave you.
LITTLE PRINCE. It is wrong for you to be here. You will suffer.
AVIATOR. I will not leave you.
LITTLE PRINCE. It's not worth the trouble.
AVIATOR. I will not leave you.

THE LITTLE PRINCE – the play

she has only enough poison for
will be very nice. I, too, shall look
s will be wells pouring out fresh
That will be so nice! You will
on little bells laughing and I will
on springs of fresh water... *(LIT-
hing more.)* Let me go on by myself. You know my flower. I am responsible for her. She has four thorns, of no use at all, to protect herself against all the world. There now... I am ready.

(AVIATOR watches helplessly as LITTLE PRINCE slowly walks trance-like toward the swaying SNAKE. At the same time, ENSEMBLE returns as "stars" and frame the SNAKE and LITTLE PRINCE. When he arrives he stands bravely by the SNAKE. At the musical change, she bites him on the ankle and disappears. LITTLE PRINCE's arms slowly raise up and he starts to fall backwards in slow motion—as depicted in St. Exupéry's picture in the book. ENSEMBLE slowly creates a wall of stars in front of LITTLE PRINCE, masking the end of his fall. Music and lights fade to black. At the last moment, the lights of ENSEMBLE's stars are extinguished in unison.)

EPILOGUE

(Lights come up slowly on AVIATOR alone on stage against a starry sky. He addresses the audience.)

AVIATOR. It is already six years since my friend went away from me with his sheep, and I have never yet told anyone this story until today. I have a selfish reason for

THE LITTLE PRINCE – the play

telling you though. It is to make sure that I never forget him. To forget a friend is sad. Not everyone has had a friend. And if I forget him I might once again become like the grown-ups. *(Beat. [Tape Cue #35])* It's true, you know. He kept his promise. At night I love to listen to the stars because to me they sound like five hundred million little bells. But there is one extraordinary thing. I realized that I never drew a strap for the muzzle—so he would never be able to fasten it on his sheep. So now I keep wondering, what if the sheep has eaten his rose? At one time I say to myself, "Surely he watches over his sheep very carefully," and then there is laughter in the stars. But at another time I say, "Perhaps the sheep got out of its box," and I wonder, and I worry. And no grown-up will ever understand that this is so important. *(He takes out his drawing pad. We watch him draw Illustration S.)* This, to me, is the loveliest and saddest landscape in the world. It is here that the little prince appeared on Earth and disappeared. Look at it carefully so that you will be sure to recognize it in case you travel some day to the African desert. And, if you should come upon this spot, please do not hurry on. Wait for a time, exactly under the star. Then, if a little man appears who laughs, who has golden hair and who refuses to answer questions, you will know who he is. If this should happen, please let me know he has come back.

(He gathers up his pad. He walks upstage as music continues. We hear the distant laughter of the LITTLE PRINCE mixed with tinkling bells. He smiles sadly, and reaches toward the starry sky.)

THE END

TABLE OF ILLUSTRATIONS

OVERHEAD PROJECTOR SETUP .... A
BOA CONSTRICTOR .... B
BOA CONSTRICTOR WITH ELEPHANT C
PLANE .... D
RAM .... E
OLD SHEEP .... F
BOX .... G
ROSE 1 .... H
ROSE 2 I
KING .... J
CONCEITED MAN .... K
LAMPLIGHTER L
LITTLE PRINCE WITH SNAKE .... M
MUZZLE .... N
DESERT FLOWER .... O
MOUNTAINS .... P
ROAD .... Q
FOX .... R
TWO DUNES WITH STAR .... S
LITTLE PRINCE IN CAPE .... T

IMPORTANT: READ CAREFULLY

NOTES ON THE SKETCH ARTIST

The role of the offstage sketch artist is an important one but it need not be difficult. The drawings displayed in this table are very simple and many of them appear in the show already partially or entirely pre-drawn. They are presented here with a numerical key which indicates the order in which the lines should be drawn. This is to simplify the task of synchronizing the strokes of the artist with those of the AVIATOR on stage. The effect is stunning but does require some rehearsal to be completely successful.

Although any number of methods can be used, the projection technique we suggest is that of an ordinary overhead projector, some acetates, and washable markers so that the acetates may be reused. It is easy and inexpensive. You should try, however, to install a dimmer to your projector so the drawings can fade up and down. Illustration A shows the setup of this rear projection method. Any fabric that will take light such as muslin or parachute fabric or rip-stop nylon can serve as a screen and backdrop.

As to the projection, the distance from the projector to the screen is approximately the same as the size of the image that will appear. For instance, if the projector is placed six feet behind the screen a six foot (measured diagonally) image will be thrown. Finally, attention should be paid to the fact that sometimes these cues are also coordinated with music as indicated in the script.

ILLUSTRATION A.

NOTE: When drawing on the overhead projector, figures will be reversed, left to right, when they are projected.

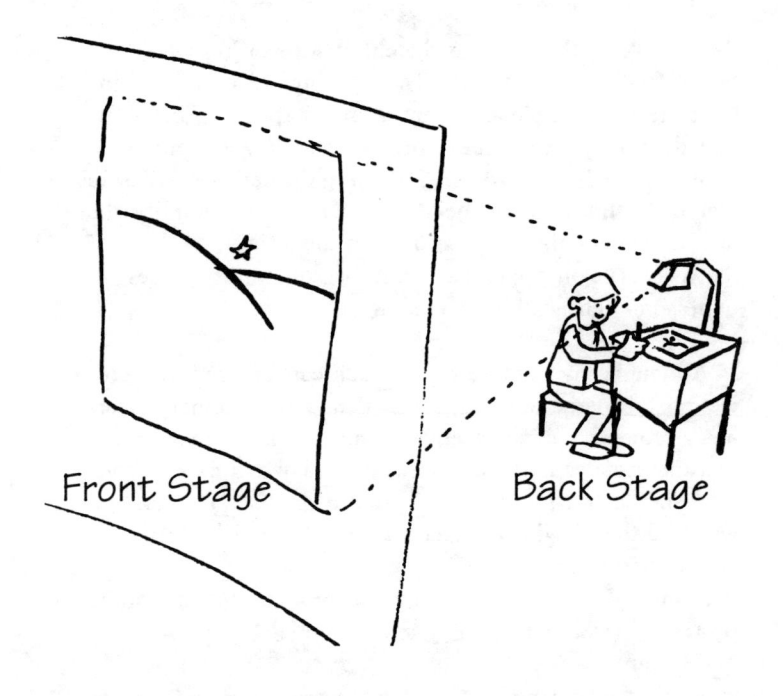

Front Stage

Back Stage

The following 20 illustrations may be photocopied and enlarged for projection. This text is completely protected by copyright. These 20 illustrations are the only part of this text which may be copied in any way, and then only for use as projections in conjunction with productions of the play.

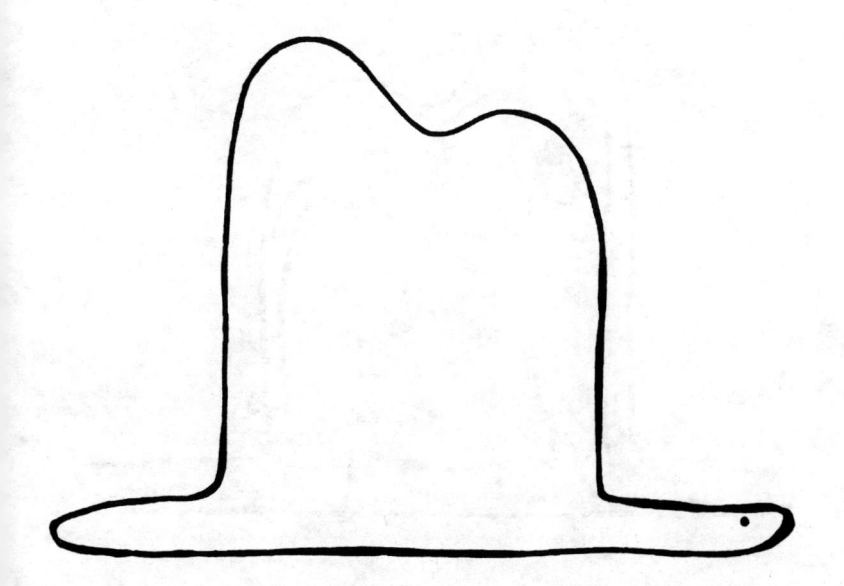

ILLUSTRATION B.

Drawing sequence:

1. Draw Outline.
2. Draw eye last.

ILLUSTRATION C.

Drawing sequence:

1. Outline Snake.
2. Elephant
3. End on Elephant's tail.

ILLUSTRATION D.

This drawing may be used if no set piece
suggesting a plane is used.

The AVIATOR may sit on a stool
in front of drawing and coordinate his movements
with the backstage sketch artist
who can simply move the acetate around
to simulate flight.

ILLUSTRATION E.

Drawing Sequence:
1. Head. 2. Body.
3. Tail. 4. Ears 5. Legs
6. Eyes <u>without eyeballs</u>.
7. Nose and Mouth.

PAUSE, then draw
8. Horns.
9. Eyeballs.

ILLUSTRATION F.

Drawing sequence:

1. Head. 2. Body. 3. Tail.
4. Ears. 5. Legs.
6. Eyes, Nose, Mouth
7. Eyeballs <u>Last.</u>

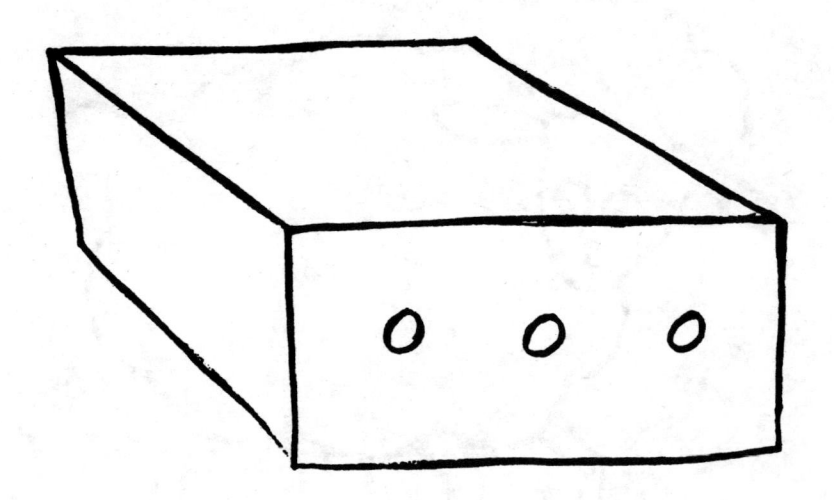

ILLUSTRATION G.

Drawing direction:
BOX - drawn fast as if angry.

ILLUSTRATION H.

Drawing sequence: 1. Petals. 2. Stem. 3. Ground—
Projector fades out.

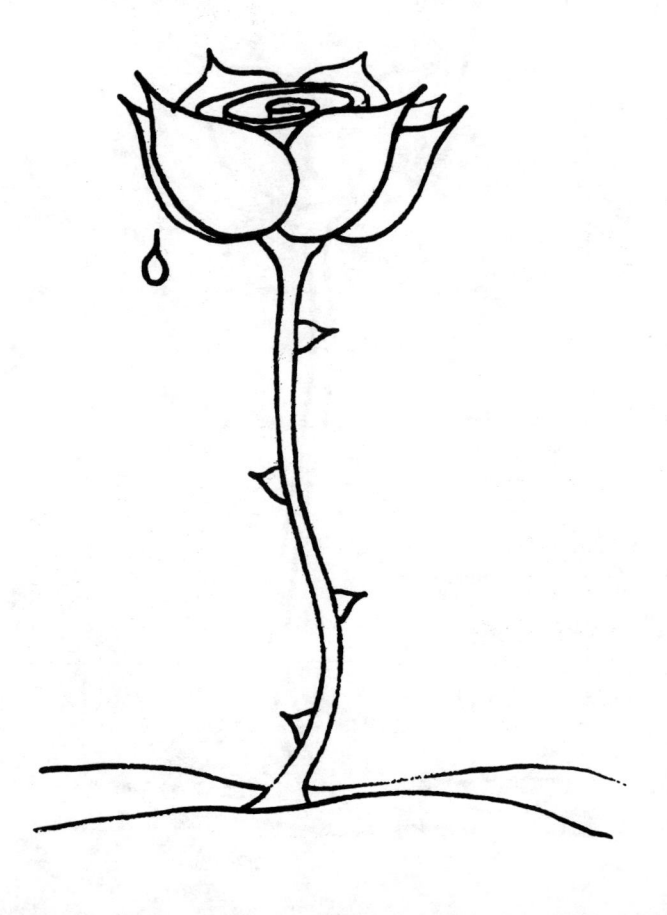

ILLUSTRATION I.

Projector comes up— ROSE is finished.
Add: 1. Thorns. 2. A couple of petals.
Tear is drawn on last note of song.

ILLUSTRATION J.

Drawing comes up fully drawn.
Just add some stars on robe.

ILLUSTRATION K

Projector comes up.
Man is drawn,
just add hat.

ILLUSTRATION L.

Drawing sequence:
Have 3 stars drawn <u>before</u> projector comes up.
1. Planet. 2. Sun. 3. Sparkle of light. 4. Man.
5. Connect Lamplighter's rod to sparkle
on final note of song.

ILLUSTRATION M.

Drawing sequence:
Projector comes up. PRINCE already drawn.

Just add SNAKE at:
"you know, you shouldn't talk to snakes..."

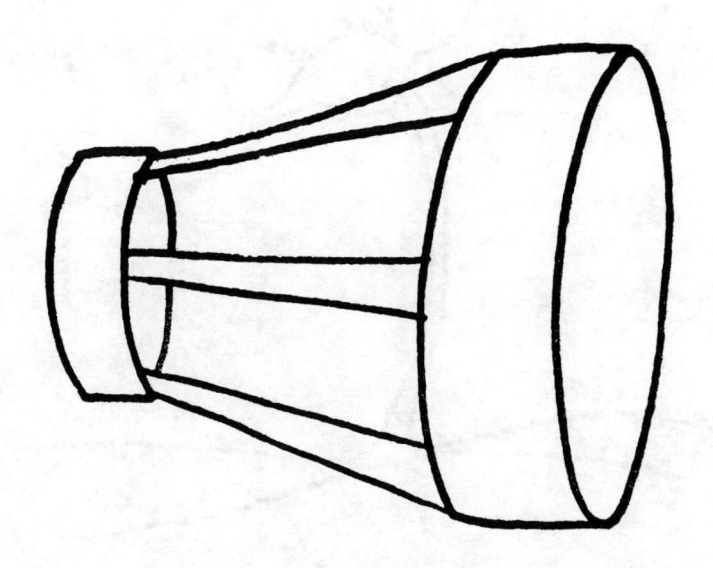

ILLUSTRATION N.

Drawing sequence:
Muzzle— Drawn <u>very fast</u>!

1. Large end.
2. Small end.
3. Connector strips.

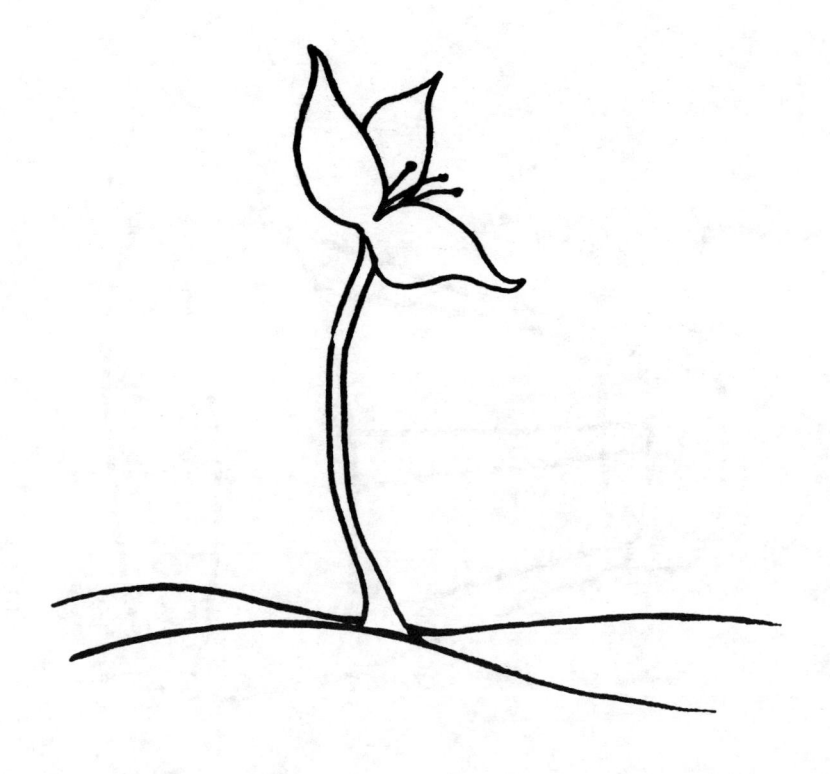

ILLUSTRATION O.

Drawing sequence: 1. Start with ground on
CUE: "After I crossed the desert..."
2. Continue upwards drawing flower.

ILLUSTRATION P.

Drawing sequence: 1. Start with mountain on...
CUE: "After that, I climbed a high mountain!"
2. Continue with sun.
3. Pointy rocks.

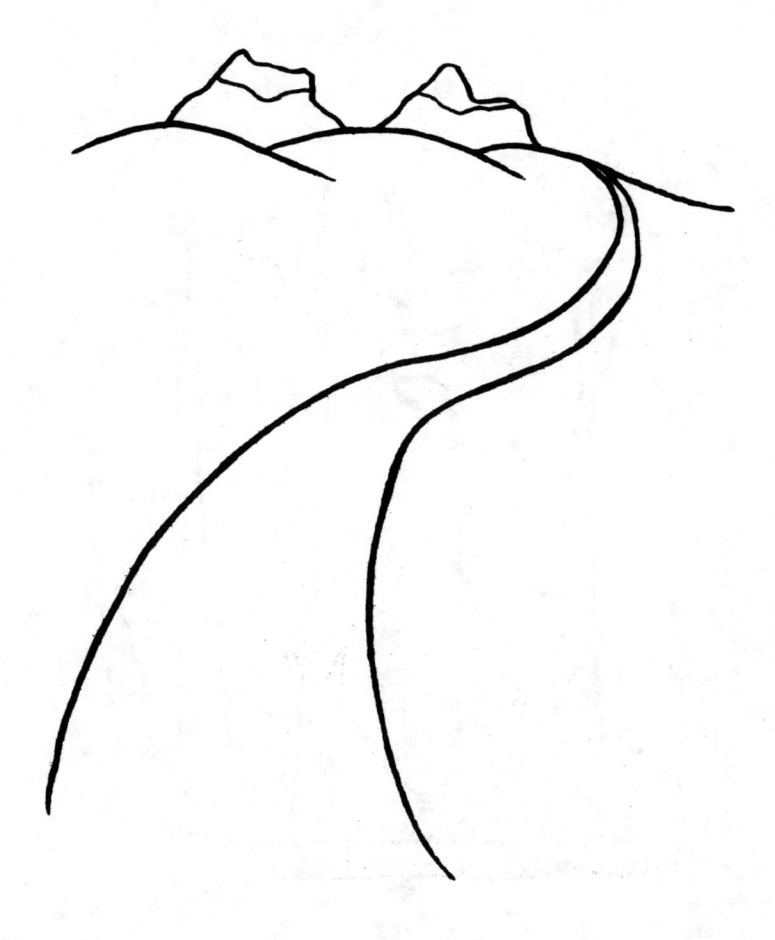

ILLUSTRATION Q.

Drawing sequence: 1. Ground. 2. Mountains. 3. Road.

ILLUSTRATION R.

Projector comes up— everything is drawn.
Just add apple.

ILLUSTRATION 5.

Drawing sequence:
1. Long curve.
2. Short curve.
3. Star.

ILLUSTRATION T.

Comes up fully drawn in full color.

ILLUSTRATION U.

Blank template to be colored as shown in illustration T.

Incidental Music Tape Cues
(All music composed and arranged by Rick Cummins)

1. Solo Voice (Prologue)
2. Solo Voice (Prologue)
3. Solo Voice (Prologue)
4. The Storm
5. Aviator Draws the "Hat"
6. Aviator Draws the Ram
7. Aviator Draws the Old Sheep
8. Scene Transition
9. Sunset Music
10. Snake Rattle
11. Little Prince Appears Again
12. Birth of the Rose
13. Fingers Touch
14. Underscore Rose and Little Prince Goodbye Scene
15. Aviator Angry, Then Begins to Draw Rose
16. Segue to King
17. Segue to Conceited Man
18. Segue to Businessman
19. Segue to Lamplighter
20. Segue to Geographer
21. The Snake
22. Snake Confronts Aviator/Little Prince Argues with Aviator
23. Little Prince Cries
24. Snake Rattle and Solo Voice
25. Underscore Aviator's Apology to Little Prince
26. Desert Flower/Mountain Echo/Wall of Roses/Segue to Fox
27. Fox Scampers Again
28. Little Prince Tames Fox
29. Little Prince Returns to Wall of Roses/Fox's Secret
30. Walk in the Desert
31. Little Prince Repeats Fox's Secret to Aviator
32. Aviator Carries Little Prince and Finds the Well
33. Plane Starts/Aviator Finds Little Prince with Snake
34. Little Prince Says Goodbye /Little Prince's Final Return to Snake
35. Epilogue

DIRECTOR'S NOTES

DIRECTOR'S NOTES

DIRECTOR'S NOTES

DIRECTOR'S NOTES

DIRECTOR'S NOTES

DIRECTOR'S NOTES

DIRECTOR'S NOTES